365 Ways

to Love

your Lover

365 Ways

to Love

your Lover

D. H. LOVE

Wings Books
New York

Copyright © 1995 by D. H. Love

All rights reserved.
This 1995 edition is published by Wings Books, a division of
Random House Value Publishing, Inc., 201 East 50th Street,
New York, New York 10022.   http://www.randomhouse.com/

by arrangement with the author.

Random House
New York · Toronto · London · Sydney · Auckland
Printed and bound in Mexico

Library of Congress Cataloging in Publication Data
Love, D. H.
365 ways to love your lover / D. H. Love.
        p.   cm.
ISBN-0-517-14872-2
1. Man-woman relationships—Miscellanea. 2. Love—Miscellanea.
        I. Title.
HQ801.L6516   1995   95-21438
        306.7—dc20   CIP

Illustrations by Sally Mara Sturman
Book design by Nancy Kenmore

8 7 6 5 4 3

Introduction

♡

Whether you're seriously involved with someone,
on the verge of a serious relationship, or just starting
out, this book will give you all the tools of the trade to
make your relationship work for you. Filled with tips,
reminders, and imaginative love games, *365 Ways to
Love your Lover* is guaranteed to perk up your love life
in ways you've never even dreamed possible.

With one tip for every day of the year, get ready to
watch your love life improve dramatically.

1 *Wake up with a smile on your face.*

2 Take a day off from work...together.

3 *When she opens up,*
listen with your heart.

4 Never tell an embarrassing story about him in front of his friends. His friends will never let him live it down and, by association, he'll never let you live it down either.

5 *When she's embarrassed, don't laugh at her— give her a hug instead.*

6 Knock before you enter the bathroom.

7 *Slip a love note in his jacket pocket.*

8 Leave a note under her pillow.

9 Make her breakfast in bed.

10 *Don't tell his mother everything.*

11 Do tell his mother some things.

12 *Call him at work and give him a love bite — he'll be working up his appetite all afternoon.*

13   Don't tell your best friend things about your partner that you would hate having his best friend know about you.

14   *Send her a racy card at work and write* "PERSONAL" *on the outside.*

15   Send him flowers.

16   *Buy her expensive perfume and then take time exploring all her pulse points.*

17  *Set aside thirty minutes of quiet time every day after work and on the weekend for pure one-on-one, unadulterated talk.*

18 If you have kids, don't argue in front of them.

19 *Buy lotions—the works—and give each other an hour-long full body massage.*

20 Go out to breakfast or brunch together, after a good night of loving.

21 *Don't criticize in public;
discuss what bothers you in private.*

22 Read each other love poems in bed.

23 *Give each other a foot massage before work.*

24 Give him a manicure.

25 *Give her a pedicure.*

26 ♯ Play romantic music during dinner.

27 *Buy him that little gadget or tool he's always wanted.*

28 Listen to each other's dreams.

29 *Be encouraging.*

30 Listen when she's had a hard day, you're not the only one.

31 *Give him one bonafide compliment a day. (Remember, if you can't say something nice, a kiss will suffice.)*

32 Occasionally. . . silence can be intriguing.

33 *Learn how to say* "I LOVE YOU" *in several different languages.*

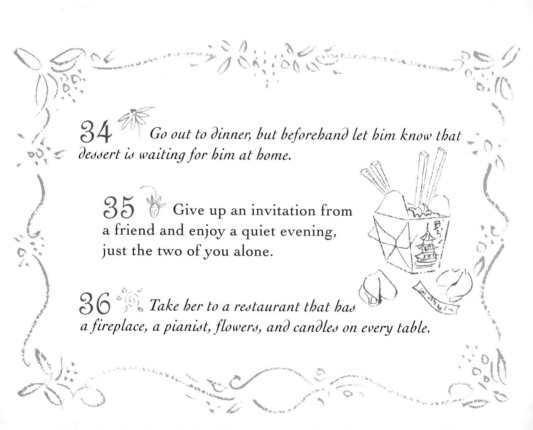

34 *Go out to dinner, but beforehand let him know that dessert is waiting for him at home.*

35 Give up an invitation from a friend and enjoy a quiet evening, just the two of you alone.

36 *Take her to a restaurant that has a fireplace, a pianist, flowers, and candles on every table.*

37 Rent a sexy movie and watch it together.

38 *Rent a sexy movie, watch it alone, then recreate your favorite scene, together. Pretend you're being judged for an Oscar on your performance. Give good directions.*

39 Call her in the middle of the night and tell her that you *love* her.

40 *Call him in the middle of the day and tell him that you* want *him.*

41 *Pack his favorite lunch to take to work and write him a "special" note on the napkin.*

42 Play a sport together.

43 *Tell her one important thing you've never told anyone else before.*

44 See if she'll do the same.

45 *Be yourself.*

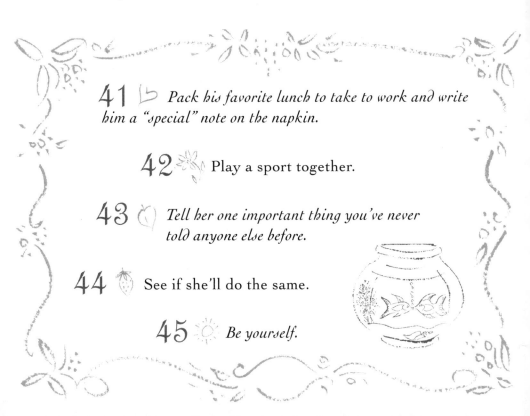

46 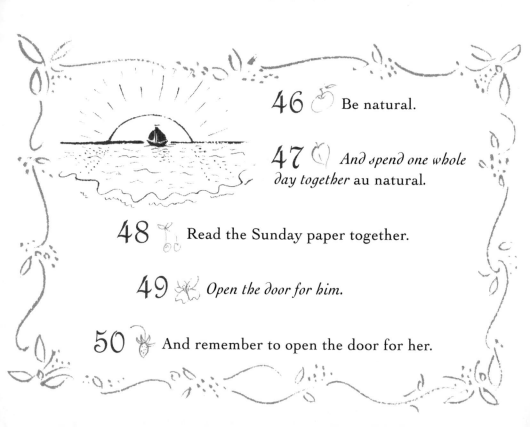 Be natural.

47 *And spend one whole day together* au natural.

48 Read the Sunday paper together.

49 *Open the door for him.*

50 And remember to open the door for her.

51 *Pick the lint off of his shirt, his sweater, his blazer. Show him you care about his appearance, too.*

52 Learn a really funny joke and spring it on her.

53 *Bring him your favorite condoms.*

54 Make a date to meet each other somewhere, and pretend it's the first time you've met.

55 *Set your alarm and watch the sun rise together.*

56 Watch the moon set together.

57 *Find a place outdoors where there is no light. Look at the stars together.*

58 Light candles and serve wine even with the simplest of meals.

59 Use cloth napkins every now and then. They're elegant and very romantic.

60 *Get all the trimmings for a picnic and ask your love to meet you for lunch. Keep the picnic a surprise.*

61 Never talk about the physical attributes of someone else.

62 *Do talk about each other's.*

63 Don't talk, listen.

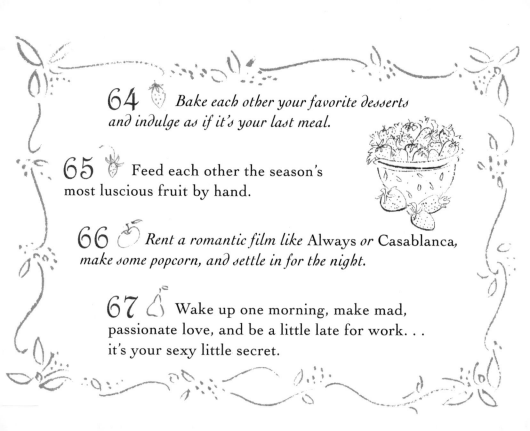

64 *Bake each other your favorite desserts and indulge as if it's your last meal.*

65 Feed each other the season's most luscious fruit by hand.

66 *Rent a romantic film like* Always *or* Casablanca, *make some popcorn, and settle in for the night.*

67 Wake up one morning, make mad, passionate love, and be a little late for work. . . it's your sexy little secret.

68 Share a piece of chocolate in a long, passionate kiss.

69 *Remember that anger impedes sexuality. Kiss and make up.*

70 Angry? Count to ten, then give her a hug.

71 *Touch often.*

72 Buy her some scented bubble bath.

73 *Run him a bath and light the room with candles. Make your own electricity.*

74 Get into the bubble bath together.

75 *Slow dance to your favorite romantic music at home.*

76 *Have a different piece of lingerie for every day of the week, plus one you keep as a surprise. Don't make the mistake of saving it for a rainy day.*

77 Tell him you think he's the sexiest man alive.

78 *Buy him a new cologne. One that drives you wild.*

79 One morning, ask her if you can blow-dry her hair.

80 *Help her put on her makeup before a special night out. Apply lipstick. Kiss, then reapply.*

81 Try dressing each other.

82 *Exercise together.*

83 Plan a surprise weekend getaway. (It needn't be costly.)

84 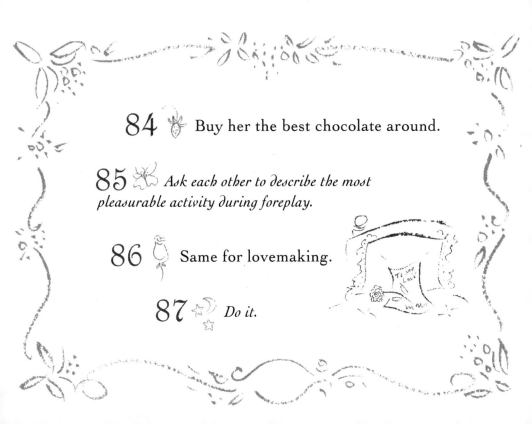 Buy her the best chocolate around.

85 *Ask each other to describe the most pleasurable activity during foreplay.*

86 Same for lovemaking.

87 *Do it.*

88 Hold hands walking down the street.

89 *Hold hands in the movies, whether they're scary or not.*

90 Write your lover an exquisite heartfelt love letter that's worth framing.

91 *Do a private dance for him.*

92 *Give each other pictures of yourselves that you really like.*

93 Plan to seduce each other. Paraphernalia is allowed.

94 *Give her the most perfect single red rose.*

95 Read a sexy romance, then tell him about it.

96 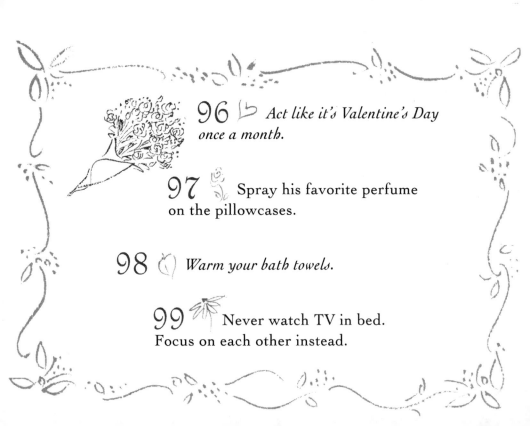 *Act like it's Valentine's Day once a month.*

97 Spray his favorite perfume on the pillowcases.

98 *Warm your bath towels.*

99 Never watch TV in bed. Focus on each other instead.

100 Appreciate your partner's strengths. Celebrate your differences.

101 *Make fresh-squeezed orange juice and warm homemade muffins for the ultimate weekend breakfast.*

102 Pretend that it's your last night together, forever.

103 *Indulge her crankiness that time of the month. . . she'll indulge you on your cranky days.*

104 Kiss each other goodnight, every night before you go to sleep.

105 *Cuddle in the morning.*

106 Leave a trail of rose petals leading from the front door into the bedroom. Light the room with candles, chill the wine, and get ready for one romantic evening.

107 *Learn how to tie his tie.*

108 *On seven pieces of paper, write seven "wish list" items you'd love for him to do to you or for you. Have him do the same. Put them in a bowl and pick one each morning before you head off to work. You have twenty-four hours to fulfill that day's command.*

109 Take a bottle of champagne to bed with you.

110 *Plan on making your partner a first priority.*

111  Let the children sleep over
with a friend or relative on your birthday.

112 *Don't let your pride get in the way
of your relationship.*

113 Never treat your partner like a child.

114 *Try going to religious services together.*

115 *Don't blame.*

116 Don't lie.

117 *Do trust.*

118 Do compliment.

119 *Have humor.*

120 Make Thursday night date night. It's a terrific prelude to the weekend.

121 *Treat your partner like a king or queen while in the company of family.*

122 Be supportive in success *and* failure.

123 *If one party owes an apology, don't make it any harder to apologize than it needs to be.*

124 *Admit that you're wrong sometimes.*

125 Give each other a kiss when you leave for work in the morning.

126 *Don't look through his wallet.*

127 Don't look through private things in general. They're private for a reason.

128 Invite her friends along; it's a sign of security. And a sign that while you may not like them, you respect each other's choices.

129 *Respect yourself.*

130 Treat your partner as you like to be treated.

131 *Let him know you'll always be there — lending an ear, a hand, your heart.*

132 *Learn the names of each other's friends.*

133 Remember nobody's perfect. . . .

134 *And that humility goes a long way.*

135 Be playful.

136 *Never order your partner around. Your partner is your equal, not your servant.*

137 Remember that if things are really messy on the outside (like an apartment), chances are that maybe something's wrong on the inside. Don't be afraid to ask "why;" don't be afraid of the answer. In talking and listening, you stand to become closer than ever.

138 *Play a game together such as* Scrabble. *Remember it's not whether you win or lose, it's how you play the game. Bend the rules a little and make it amorous. Whoever wins gets the choice to. . . . This way you may both end up winners.*

139 *Call his mom or sister and make the connection. It could pay off in a big way.*

140 Never preach to your partner (it's a big turn-off!). Offer up suggestions instead; they're much easier to swallow.

141 *Do ask for directions when you're lost.*

142 Help each other when there's something really important to be accomplished.

143 *Sharing is caring.*

144 When you aim to hurt, remember you may be hurting yourself even more.

145 *Think before you act.*

146 Trust does not come overnight. Build it and it will come.

147 *Remember that today is today and tomorrow is tomorrow. Neither one can be repeated.*

148 ☆ Don't generalize about your partner's behavior. Try to be specific. It's a much more effective way of getting to the root of the problem.

149 *Instead of confrontation, think of a better way to get your point across.*

150 Have a day with absolutely nothing scheduled. Enjoy the complete down-time together and let unexpected events come your way.

151 *Get perspective and try on the other shoe every now and again.*

152 Tell each other your greatest romantic fantasy. Make a date to act it out.

153 *Don't try to recreate that special moment you remember. Make new memories.*

154 Never *act out* your jealousy. Try to talk it through instead.

155 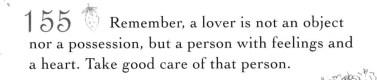 Remember, a lover is not an object nor a possession, but a person with feelings and a heart. Take good care of that person.

156 *Time alone can be a good thing. Time together is even better.*

157 Don't try to compete with each other's outside interests. Learn about them, and make them your friends.

158 Don't nag. If you don't get satisfaction, ask to sit down quietly for a talk.

159 *Build a fire and snuggle up in front of it.*

160 Go camping and lie under the stars.

161 *If you share a bank account, really share it.*

162 *Never act upon guilt. The act won't feel good to you and probably won't feel genuine to the recipient either.*

163 Honor your promises.

164 *Never whine. It's thoroughly unbecoming.*

165 Buy a pet together—and share responsibilities.

166 *Hold a theme party—be creative together.*

167 *Go to a flea market. You never know what buried treasure you may discover together.*

168 Go to a museum together. Seek out one particular artist or one significant work. Make it like a treasure hunt; the winner gets a very *hot* kiss or you can create your own rules for the winner.

169 *Don't use the past as a weapon.*

170 Clip out an article that you think may be of interest. Appeal to her mind as well.

171   Good hygiene is very important.

172   *Take a shower together before lovemaking.*
You're both refreshed, relaxed, and ready for action.

173   Take a sunset walk together at the beach.
If you're not near a beach,
find the nearest lake.

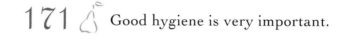

174   *Go for a sunrise jog*
together around the neighborhood.

175 Pamper yourself and you'll set a good example.

176 *Buy a really luxurious shampoo and conditioner. Lather up, then give each other a soothing or vigorous scalp massage, whichever suits the mood.*

177 Do what you say you're going to do. Follow through with your commitments.

178 *One drink is nice; too many might spoil your senses.*

179 *Before you point the finger, consider your partner might already know a mistake has been made, and may already have found a way to make up for it.*

180 Arguments are okay. Remember, making up is the fun part.

181 *Keep pet names all to yourselves.*

182 Television tends to tune out the senses, but a deep stare, a languorous kiss, and a soft caress can restore the balance.

183 *Try not to bear a grudge,* bare yourself instead.

184 Buy take-out Chinese food and eat it in bed, naked.

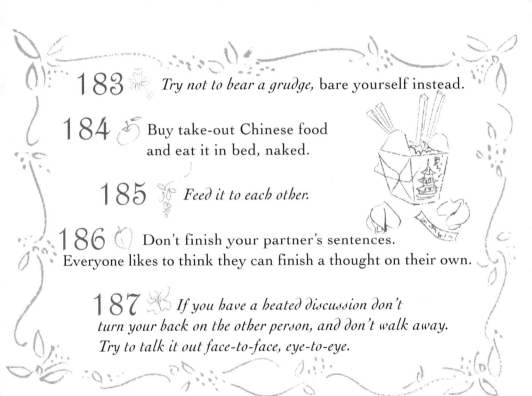

185 *Feed it to each other.*

186 Don't finish your partner's sentences. Everyone likes to think they can finish a thought on their own.

187 *If you have a heated discussion don't turn your back on the other person, and don't walk away. Try to talk it out face-to-face, eye-to-eye.*

188

Undying	**L**asting
Neverending	**O**nly
Consummate	**V**ast
One	**E**vermore
Nirvana	
Dearest	
Invincible	
Total	
Irreversible	
Omnipotent	
Normal	
Actual	
Love	

189 *Make time to be with each other.*

190 Don't interrupt when your partner is speaking.

191 *Buy some film and shoot an entire roll of each other. Make a collage of photos as a keepsake.*

192 Be goofy.

193 *Laugh a lot.*

194   If you have something important to say, be direct.

195   *Clean the bathroom sink after you shave.*

196   In general, leave the bathroom clean for the next person.

197   *Pick a charity you both want to fund; charity opens the door to the heart.*

198 When conflict arises, talk until you find a solution that's good for both of you.

199 *The three "R's" you don't want to learn:*

(1) *Routine*

(2) *Regular*

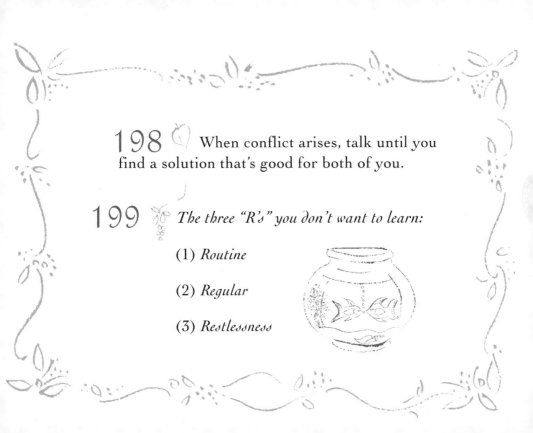

(3) *Restlessness*

200 *In times of trouble, turn to each other first before you approach a friend.*

201 Play with her hair.

202 *Run your fingers through his hair. Do it again.*

203 An idea can be as precious as a gift; look inside, inspect it, try it on for size.

204 *Ask him to marry you again.*

205 Synchronize your watches.

206 *Don't worry about the neighbors.*

207 Pick a hobby you both like, pursue it together.

208 Reminisce about the first time you met.

209 *Reminisce about the first time you fell in love.*

210 Treat each other with the same courtesy you did as the first time you met.

211 *Sweep her off her feet. Literally.*

212 Make friends feel welcome.
The good feeling will spread.

213 *Look at your lover's face when you're speaking;*
it's much nicer than staring at the ceiling or the wall.

214 Remember your anniversary.

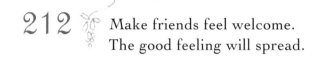

215 *Go without makeup and jewelry for a whole*
weekend, and let the uninhibited feeling take over.

216 *Throw your partner a surprise birthday party.*

217 Don't flirt with the opposite sex. Give your lover your undivided attention.

218 *Go food shopping together. It can be a very seductive experience, with a little imagination.*

219 Shower your partner with affection.

220 *Pick your partner's favorite physical attribute. Find a way to show how much you like it.*

221 When you go clothes shopping, buy him something—even if it's a tie or a funky pair of socks.

222 *Never tell your partner about a surprise you were planning, but were unable to carry through. Save your idea for the next time.*

223 If you like yourself, it shows, and will make your partner even more attracted to you.

224 Follow one of your partner's suggestions, and show that you respect her opinion.

225 *Show your appreciation by wearing or displaying a gift you've received from your partner.*

226 Kiss, hug, rub often. Touching is a vital act.

227 *Never go to bed angry.*

228 Make piña coladas and pretend you're on a tropical island together. Go with the fantasy. . . .

229 *Don't make idle threats. Don't threaten, period. It's a turn-off!*

230 Don't bring work into the bedroom; make this room your sanctuary.

231 *Do something totally uncharacteristic and unpredictable with or for your loved one.*

232 *Fool around in the back of a cab or car. You're not driving so make it a ride worth remembering.*

233 Go to a drive-in movie and make yourselves comfortable in the back seat.

234 *Buy a pair of spike black patent leather shoes. Put them on. . .and that's all you need for the night.*

235 Have fun exploring and searching for the illustrious "G-spot."

236 Blow in his warm, wet ear, and see how he responds.

237 *Play lip service with your lips only.*

238 Don't be petty. Have a big heart instead.

239 *Schedule shared activities.*

240 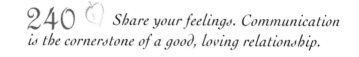 *Share your feelings. Communication
is the cornerstone of a good, loving relationship.*

241 Be honest.

242 *Validate his concerns; offer comfort
and a reassuring word or touch.*

243 Don't argue in front of family
members that don't live with you.

244 *Take a champagne bath.*

245 Take a bottle of champagne into the bath.

246 *Try to be involved in decisions. If you're indifferent, you run the risk of being left out and feeling angry afterwards.*

247 Seize the moment.

248 *Never fake an orgasm.*

249 ☀ Let your hair down! Literally.

250 🦋 *Plan a night out on the town doing things you both agree upon.*

251 ☽ Check into a local hotel or motel for the weekend or just a night.

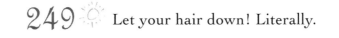

252 🌿 *Play around a lot.*

253  Go to an adult-only store together and pick out one totally outrageous item. Have fun.

254 *Hint: Buy a feather and use it during foreplay.*

255 Let go all the way.

256 *Try to stimulate more than one erogenous zone at a time.*

257 *Practice staying limber.*

258 Be open with your partner about pleasure spots. You may even find some new ones while exploring!

259 *Shower your partner with praise, even if it's just because dinner tastes better than usual.*

260 Walk down the street with your arms around each other's waists, and bring yourselves physically closer to each other.

261 *Spend an entire weekend catering to each other's needs.* EXAMPLE: *Begin with breakfast in bed, end with a warm sponge bath. The rest is up to you!*

262 Notice the little things your partner does for you and show your appreciation. (Saying "thank you" is a nice place to start.)

263 *Don't keep secrets from each other.*

264 Be sensitive to each other's needs.

265 Take her in your arms and tell her how much you love her.

266 *If you're going to do a favor, do it graciously.*

267 Have an afternoon rendezvous with your lover.

268 *Feel proud of the partner you've chosen to be with.*

269 If you think you're going to be late, call.

270 *Don't act out your aggressions on your partner. Talk about your problem.*

271 Tell your partner how much he or she turns you on.

272 *Spend time in a kiss, exploring, nibbling, and getting to know every square inch of your partner's delicious mouth.*

273 Try a new position.

274 Buy a book on Kama Sutra.

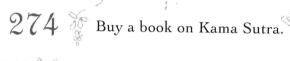

275 *After a hard day's work, offer to cook dinner or bring home take-out.*

276 If you're taking a walk together, whether in the country or on the beach, gather some keepsakes from nature and display them at home. You will always have a concrete memory of that cherished relaxing time.

277 *Agree beforehand on a weekend day when all conversations will be "work-free."*

278 *If your partner has a health problem, be sensitive and try to help when you can.*

279 Be faithful, always.

280 *Go apartment or house hunting together. Spend some time talking about your perfect dream home.*

281 Let him watch sports. And agree ahead of time to spend a day or evening doing what you want to do.

282 Let him know he's your best friend.

283 *Let her know she's your best friend.*

284 Take him to a restaurant he's always wanted to visit.

285 *Take her to the opera she's always dreamed of seeing.*

286 Tell him it's his day off.

287 *Tell her it's her day off.*

288 Mind and matter are equally important.
So respect both, please.

289 *Couples that shower together, stay together.*

290 *Devote time to your lovemaking.*

291 And be gentle in your lovemaking.

292 *Tickle each other.*

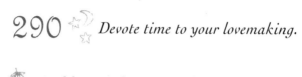

293 Find your partner's pleasure spot.

294 *Cuddle after you make love.*

295 Pick a favorite love song
and make it your song.

296 *If you go away on business, make the first
night back a special night with your sexiest lingerie.*

297 Don't ignore your partner
when she's speaking to you.

298 *Pay attention to the details.*

299 *If you keep a diary, share it with your partner every now and then.*

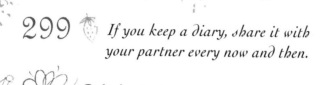

300 Carry a picture of your partner around in your wallet.

301 *If he has a favorite breakfast food, buy it for him. It'll be the first thing he eats and he'll think of you all day long.*

302 Buy a gift your partner might wear often like a scarf or a tie or a piece of jewelry. This way when it's put on, you will come to mind.

303 *Buy a piece of art together, it needn't be expensive and will be infused with both of your tastes.*

304 Keep air freshener in the bathroom.

305 *Use moisturizer after showering. Smooth skin is very sexy.*

306 Buy fresh flowers for no occasion but to say, "I love you."

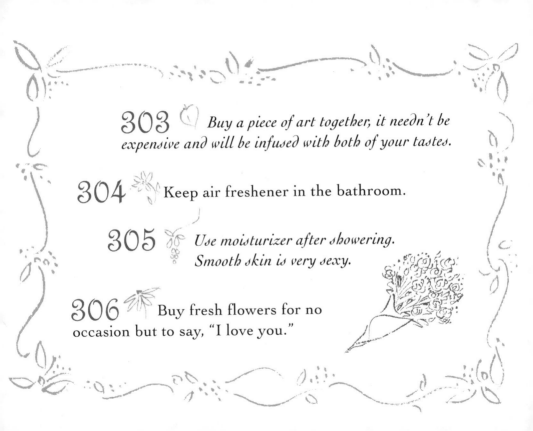

307 Don't accept phone calls after 10 p.m. unless it's an emergency.

308 *If your partner is more sensitive than usual to something you've said or done, be understanding.*

309 Don't say something you might regret five minutes later.

310 *Learn how to perfect your kiss. Practice makes perfect.*

311   Hold the umbrella for her when it's raining.

312   *If you're not holding anything,
help her carry her bags.*

313   Whisper sweet somethings in her ear.

314   *Prominently display a photo of
your loved one at work.*

315 *Don't put your partner down. Lift his spirits instead.*

316 Leave the dishes in the sink for tonight.

317 *Make a tape of your favorite love songs and give it to your partner.*

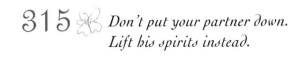

318 Stick a couple of chocolate kisses in his pocket.

319  *Buy her a huggable teddy bear.*

320 In the morning, bring her coffee or tea in bed.

321 *Help each other make dinner.*

322 Help each other wash up.

323 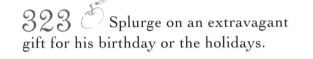 Splurge on an extravagant gift for his birthday or the holidays.

324 *Come to her defense in public.*

325 Make a fuss, even if it's a small cut.

326 *Brush your teeth before you retire for the night. A fresh mouth is a sexy mouth.*

327 Don't be a know-it-all. It's very unbecoming.

328 *Don't look at members of the opposite sex when you're with your partner.*

329 Bake him his favorite cookies or brownies and wrap them up as a gift.

330 *Write him a love poem.*

331 *Offer to help your lover's family with an important project.*

332 Be ultra-committed to each other.

333 *Keep the bedroom clean.*

334 Use floral potpourri to scent the bedroom.

335 *Spend a whole day in bed together.*

336 ♡ Don't forget Valentine's Day.

337 ♡ *Never make fun of an outfit your partner is wearing.*

338 🍓 Never mutter under your breath, unless you're prepared to be heard.

339 *Send him a piece of sexy lingerie at work. Mark the package "CONFIDENTIAL."*

340 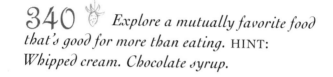 *Explore a mutually favorite food that's good for more than eating.* HINT: *Whipped cream. Chocolate syrup.*

341 Go rollerblading together.

342 *Kiss him softly and repeatedly on the eyelids.*

343 Talk dirty in bed.

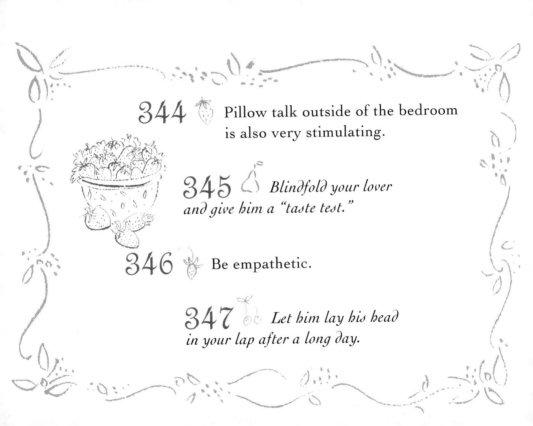

344 Pillow talk outside of the bedroom is also very stimulating.

345 *Blindfold your lover and give him a "taste test."*

346 Be empathetic.

347 *Let him lay his head in your lap after a long day.*

348 *Fall asleep in each other's arms.*

349 If you don't live together, give your lover a special "loving" wake-up call.

350 *And let him know what kind of surprise might be in store for him later.*

351 Set the table, and eat dinner in the nude.

352 *Put your dirty laundry in the basket.*

353　Don't spy on your partner.

354　*Keep your mouth open when kissing, closed when chewing.*

355　Go see a movie with your lover in the afternoon.

356　*Use breath mints if you smoke.*

357　Be emotionally available, even if you think you have something better to do. Your relationship is an investment.

358 *Save one-up-man-ship for the men.*

359 Be aware of changes in your partner, especially obvious external ones like a haircut.

360 *Be understanding of the occasional mood.*

361 Ask your partner if she wants to share what you've ordered.

362 *Don't start eating until your partner's had a chance to sit down.*

363 If you borrow a personal item, return it intact.

364 *Try to eat breakfast together.*

365 Make love all night long!